The Secret Code
on your
Hands

AN ILLUSTRATED GUIDE TO PALMISTRY

Vernon Mahabal

MANDALA
PUBLISHING

San Rafael, CA

MANDALA
PUBLISHING

PO BOX 3088
San Rafael, CA 94912
www.mandalapublishing.com

Library of Congress Cataloging-in-Publication Data available.

ISBN: 978-1-60109-004-1

ROOTS of PEACE    REPLANTED PAPER

Insight Editions, in association with Roots of Peace, will
plant two trees for each tree used in the manufacturing of
this book. Roots of Peace is an internationally renowned hu-
manitarian organization dedicated to eradicating land mines
worldwide and converting war-torn lands into productive
farms and wildlife habitats. Together, we will plant two mil-
lion fruit and nut trees in Afghanistan and provide farmers
there with the skills and support necessary for sustainable
land use.

10 9 8 7 6 5 4 3 2
Manufactured in China by Insight Editions
www.insighteditions.com

Contents

This book is dedicated to my wife, Madhavi, and my son Kanhaiya Enki.

What Is Palmistry?

Your hands contain information that explain your true talents and abilities. They express what you are good at doing and what will make you happy. Your hands explain these things in symbols, like a secret code. To learn how to read hands is to unlock this secret code. Very few people in this world know how to do this, but many great kings, queens, magicians, and conquerors of the ancient world knew how to read hands. Being a palmist is like being a detective. When you are looking at palms, you are like a private investigator who sees clues and figures out what they mean.

Think of the hand as a road map of your life. When walking around in a city, or enjoying a museum, a map is a very important item. It lets us know where we are, what we will be able to see, and the fastest way to other places. The map of our hands lets us know our own individual talents and abilities. If we learn to read our map, life will become easier for us. When we understand what we are naturally good at, we will become very strong and confident.

Some people may tell you that palmistry is supernatural, or even spooky. Only those who have no real knowledge about palmistry will say these things. There is nothing to be afraid of with palmistry. Hand reading is a science, just like the science of medicine or technology. All the great ancient civilizations taught palmistry in their schools and universities. Some people will ask you, "What if my hand says something bad?" You will be able to tell them that palmistry explains what you are good at doing, and what will make you happy. If you have difficulties, the hands will always show how to work them out. Once people start finding out that you are learning palmistry, many will want you to look at their hands and answer questions about their lives.

Learning to read hands is enjoyable, and it is something that can really help people. As you read more and more hands, you will want to learn as much as you can about palmistry. Carry this book around with you, and look up information that you need. You may also want to read other palmistry books after you have understood everything in this one. You will also learn by talking to, or even studying with, other palmists. Palmistry is a fascinating science!

How I Became a Palmist

My introduction to palmistry began when I bought a book about it that was written over one hundred years ago. It taught a very ancient form of palmistry, and reading it took me into the world of palmistry's rich history. Most of its ideas were very outdated, but I had enough information to get started.

A couple of years later, I met a palmist named Patrick who read hands at a table on St. Mark's Place in New York City. Listening to him give readings made me want to learn palmistry myself, so I read every book on the topic that I could find and looked at many different hands. Sometimes, I rode the subway and gave people readings on their way to work. I also enjoyed meeting other palmists and sharing information with them. That is how my palmistry career began.

Since then, I've read thousands of hands and given hundreds of classes. As a palmist, I've met fascinating people and traveled to many interesting places.

You can read this book to unlock the secrets of your own hands, or the hands of others, as I have done. Whichever you desire, the path of palmistry is very powerful. The more that you look at other people's hands, the more you learn about yourself. You will never get bored with palmistry.

Every person is an individual, therefore every hand is completely different. You will see or learn something new every time you study a hand. When you look into a person's palm, you are entering the gateway to their soul.

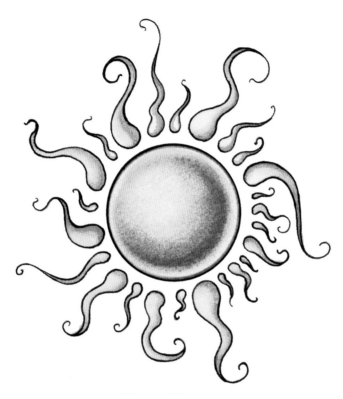

The Hand

The Hand: The Physical Landscape

HAND COLORS

The color on your palms can sometimes change. Most of the time, your palms will be a shade of pink. Now and then, your palms will change to a different color. Keep your eyes open for this. *The different colors will tell you about how a person is feeling.*

PINK: A pinkish color is normal for the palm. When it is pink, you feel good. You will also have a lot of energy, and you will feel healthy.

RED: When your palm looks reddish, it usually means that you are upset or mad at someone. Most of the time, it is because they will not let you do something that you really want to do. Watch your temper. If your hands are very red, you will feel like fighting. Exercise or play sports to get rid of your anger.

YELLOW: When you have a yellowish palm, it means that you are worrying too much about something. There is something bothering you. A very yellow palm means that you have been criticizing other people—calling them names or making fun of them. Try giving advice instead. Very yellow palms mean you really want people to listen to you.

WHITE: When your palms look a little white, you need some time alone; you might not want to talk to anyone for a while. Your friends may be wondering what's wrong. If your palms are very white, you are feeling lazy—you might just want to stay in bed all day.

BLUE: Bluish palms indicate that something's on your mind, and if your palms are very blue, you are feeling very sad. Talk to someone you love or feel very close to. Get your feelings out!

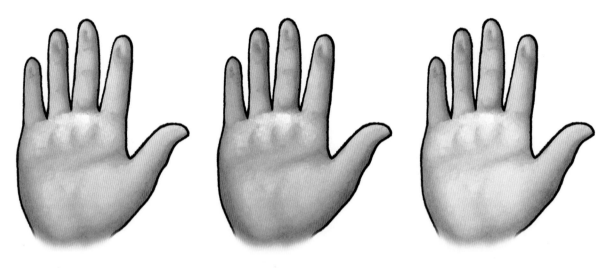

PINK HAND   RED HAND   YELLOW HAND

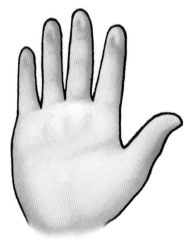

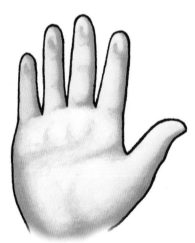

WHITE HAND   BLUE HAND

PALM SHAPES

The shape of your palm is very important because it describes your basic personality. The qualities indicated by the shape of your palm become part of your life in every way. It tells how you take part in life.

THE SQUARE PALM

(#1) If your palms look like this:

You like to spend a lot of time outdoors. Your body will usually be strong, and you may like to play sports and be active. It's not important for you to have many friends—just a few very good ones. Also, you do not like a lot of change in your life. In fact, if you can follow a regular schedule, you'll get a lot of things done. You are also probably great at building and constructing things.

#1

THE RECTANGLE PALM

(#2) If your palms look like this:

You possess a great imagination, and you probably dream a lot. Write down your ideas every day. You may even be able to write poetry or short stories. You are a very warm person to others, and you may be very emotional and sensitive at times. Your feelings are important to you. You like a lot of peace in your life, and you don't like fighting and arguing. You enjoy spending time alone. You are very loving to those you care about. People with rectangular palms are usually very artistic.

#2

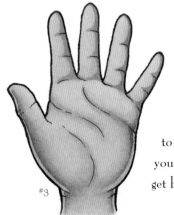

The Round Palm

(#3) If your palms look like this:

You like to have a lot of friends. You enjoy parties and entertainment.

You love meeting new people and sharing ideas with others. You also like to help people. You love attention from others. You are very open-minded, and you might work to help others later in your life. People with round palms also get bored very easily.

The Triangular Palm

(#4) If your palms look like this:

You can be a very restless person. You like to do things that are adventurous, like climbing mountains or hiking. You dislike sitting at home. You like to discover and explore all kinds of things. You are always busy and energetic. You love freedom and do not like people telling you what to do. You are also a leader, and you like to be in charge.

Are You a Righty or a Lefty? (Which Hand Do You Read?)

As you are learning to be a palmist, you may wonder which hand to look at. Do you read both hands or just one? If you are only going to look at someone's palms for a few minutes, ask them which hand they write with and read that one.

If you have more time to look at your friend's hands, then you should read both and compare them with each

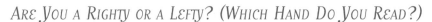

6

other. The most important hand to focus on will be their main hand. Palmists call the hand that you write with or eat with your "main" hand. For most people, the main hand will be the right one. Most people are right-handed, and it is a lot easier to be right-handed because most things are made for right hand use.

What if you or your friend is left-handed? Did you know that if you put one hundred people in a room, about fifteen of them will be left-handed? To be left-handed is very special. You should be proud if you are a lefty. As a left-hander, you have a very strong inner voice. This means that you can listen to your heart or feelings to give you the right answers. Right-handers may have this voice also, but they tend to ignore it because they don't trust it. Righties feel more comfortable when they make choices using their mind and intelligence, and left-handed people are happier following their hearts. A lefty will want to do many things differently than most. Many great artists and musicians in history were left-handed. They did many things in life their own way and became very successful.

THE BUSY HAND AND THE PEACEFUL HAND

Sometimes, a hand may be filled with lines going in every direction (#5), and it looks complicated! Palmists call this "the busy hand."

People who have many lines covering their palm have many different interests and hobbies. They like to know something about everything. Their minds are always alert to things that are going on around them. Sometimes they may find it difficult to concentrate on just one subject or hobby. They are interested in so many different things that they scatter their energy in too many directions. If you have this palm pattern, try focusing on one or two subjects that really interest you.

You may come across a palm that seems to have only three or four lines. These few lines are usually deeply cut into the hand. These are also darker in color than those of the busy hand. This hand is called "the

#5

peaceful hand" because it has fewer lines (#6).

Focusing on one or two hobbies is not difficult for those with a peaceful hand. They know what they like to do, and they do it. These people are not really interested in what the rest of the world does or in other people's ideas.

If you have this palm pattern, try to keep your mind open to other's ideas and opinions. You will see that whatever you do well, you will be able to do even better!

#6

HARD HANDS, SOFT HANDS

This section is a hands-on experience! You will need to read it two or three times while constantly checking the hardness or softness of at least five or more people's hands. I suggest that you read this section once quickly, then examine as many palms as possible. Then come back and re-read it until you get a feel for the hardness and softness of hands.

The feel, the hardness or softness, of the hand shows how we act with other people in the world. This exercise might be difficult to try on yourself. It is very easy to try on others. Place your fingers over the top of a person's hand and press your thumb right in the middle of their palm. Does the hand feel hard, medium, or soft? Don't just feel the skin; squeeze down on the whole palm!

HARD HANDS

(#7) Hard hands feel like a hard pencil eraser.

People with hard hands:
• Have lots of physical energy.

#7

• Are always busy and active.
• May spend a lot of time outdoors.
• Are very determined to get what they want.
• Can be very opinionated and not open to other people's views.
• Do not like doing things unless they can get something out of it.
• Can sometimes be stubborn or pushy.

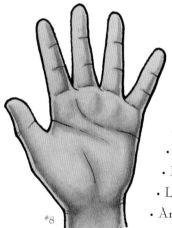

#8

MEDIUM-HARD HANDS

(#8) Medium-hard hands feel firm, like a ripe peach.

People with medium-hard hands:
• Have a healthy body.
• Get along well with others.
• Have a positive attitude.
• Like to work hard and play hard.
• Are very responsible.

SOFT HANDS

(#9) These hands feel like an overripe banana.

People with soft hands:
• Are easy-going and relaxed.
• Like to enjoy life.
• Like beautiful things and good-tasting foods.

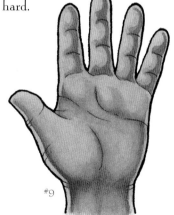

#9

• Are very helpful, warm, and sensitive to others.
• Like to do things indoors.

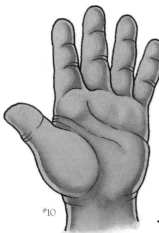

#10

VERY SOFT HANDS

(#10) Very soft hands feel squishy, like a marshmallow. You will rarely come across very soft hands.

People with very soft hands:
• Do not have a lot of physical energy.
• Like a lot of luxury and comfort.
• Are lazy, and they try to get others to do things for them.
• They may need to eat a better diet and get more exercise.

THICK HANDS, THIN HANDS

If you look at your hands from the side, you will see that they will be either thick or thin. Look at other people's hands and compare them with yours.

THIN HANDS

(#11) Thin hands belong to people who spend much time in thought. They may think about philosophy, science, or spiritual topics. Most of the time, they like peace and quiet around them. They might even be a bit shy.

#11

THICK HANDS

(#12) Thick hands belong to those who are outgoing or extroverted. They love partying, meeting people, and socializing. They are bold around others and sometimes even loud.

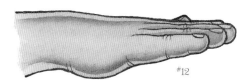

#12

If your hands are somewhere in-between, you will have some of the qualities of both the thick hand and the thin hand.

MOUNTAINS

On your palm, you will find upraised pads of flesh that palmists call "mountains." There are eight main mountains, and each has the qualities of one particular planet in our solar system. To be a true mountain, it must rise up like a little pillow and may even feel soft when you press down on it. To have a mountain on your palm means that the energy of a particular planet is within you.

Some people will have one or two mountains developed. Others will have three or four mountains. Do not worry if you see that other people have more mountains than you. It may be better to have just one or two mountains because it will be easier to focus your talents. If many of your mountains are developed, you will have many talents available to you, but it may be hard to choose which ones to pursue. People with many mountains on their palm must learn to use all of their talents together. *This is a palmistry principle: if it's large in your hand, it's large in your life.*

Compare your hand with the diagram and look at each of the eight planetary areas. Each area will either be flat or have a developed mountain. The following will explain what each mountain means to the person.

MOON MOUNTAIN

You have a very good imagination, and you are a dreamer. Put your ideas into something creative like art or painting.

VENUS MOUNTAIN

You are a very warm and friendly person. You love to go to parties and meet people. You are attracted to beautiful things like nice clothes, cars, and fine artwork.

MARS MOUNTAIN

You are a very active person. You like to play sports because you love to compete. You are also a very brave person.

JUPITER MOUNTAIN

You want to be the best at whatever you do. You may enjoy being a leader. You are a very confident person.

SATURN MOUNTAIN

You are a very serious person. You like to study and learn things. You love to collect knowledge and information. You may also enjoy spending time alone.

SUN MOUNTAIN

You are an artistic person. You are very dramatic and may love to act or be a comedian. You want attention from others and enjoy being on stage.

MERCURY MOUNTAIN

You are very good at speaking and communicating. You are very curious, and you like to know about everything around you. You may also enjoy writing.

PLUTO MOUNTAIN

You are a fighter or a warrior. You stand up for what you believe in. You don't believe in giving up.

The Fingers

The Fingers: The Forest of Talents

MERCURY · SUN · SATURN · JUPITER

THE FINGERS OF JUPITER AND THE SUN

The fingers are named after the planets because they hold the energies of the planets within them. The longer fingers are considered stronger than the others. This means that the energies of some planets are more active within you than others.

Start by comparing the length of your finger of Jupiter with your finger of the Sun. Place your hand palm down on a desk or table. Hold your fingers close together so that there are no spaces between them. Look at both your Jupiter and Sun fingers. Which is longer?

· The finger of Jupiter contains the energies of power and leadership.

· The finger of the Sun contains the energies of creativity and individuality.

LONGER JUPITER FINGER

If your finger of Jupiter is longer than your Sun finger, you have natural leadership abilities. Organizing people and giving direction to others is your greatest talent. Because you always like to be the boss, you may not like it when others tell you what to do. Many great military generals and presidents of companies have longer Jupiter fingers. People who have longer Jupiter fingers also like to help others. They like to do things that make life better for others, such as giving money or volunteering for charities. Those tendencies are more pronounced as you get older.

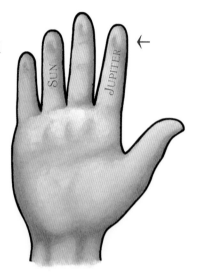

LONGER SUN FINGER

If your Sun finger is longer than your Jupiter finger, doing artistic or creative things is very important to you. Many famous musicians and artists have longer Sun fingers. Having creative hobbies—playing music, drawing, building things—makes you happy. You also like to be popular, and become bored when people do not give you enough attention. Standing out in a crowd and being different is more important to you than being in charge.

Sometimes both fingers seem equally long. If this is true for you, pick the finger that looks wider and fatter. This will be your stronger finger.

FINGERTIPS ON THE JUPITER FINGER

Jupiter is the planet of spirituality, faith, beliefs and hopes. The shape of the upper tip portion of the Jupiter finger indicates the type of spirituality that one is attracted to.

There are four fingertip shapes: Earth, Water, Fire, and Air.

1. EARTH FINGERTIP: (The Earth tip is flat on top)
You enjoy being part of an organized spiritual group or movement. You are very attracted to religious ceremonies, rituals, and old traditions. You are also inspired by large temples, cathedrals, and beautiful churches.

2. WATER FINGERTIP: (The Water tip is pointed)
The world of prophecy, intuition, and psychic energy very much interests you. You have a strong inner faith in everything spiritual and do not require proof for your beliefs. Above all, you are attracted to the devotional pastimes of love and friendship between God/Goddess and their devotees.

3. FIRE FINGERTIP: (The Fire tip looks like a small spatula)
You have very individualistic and unique spiritual views. People who create new religions or spiritual movements possess this finger shape. You may one day become a spiritual warrior or crusader.

4. AIR FINGERTIP: (The Air tip is rounded)
For you, the most important part of a spiritual path is the philosophy behind it. Reading scriptures, collecting knowledge, and discovering ancient wisdom is what you enjoy most. People with this fingertip like to see connections, rather than differences, between science and religion.

Do You Have Long Fingers or Short Fingers?

Now we will look at your fingers. It is our fingers (and thumbs) that allow us to do so many things with our hands. The palms contain many types of energies, but it is the fingers' job to bring those energies out to the world. Our fingers also bring in energies from the world around us to our palm. They thus act just like trees, which bring the energies out from the Earth and take energies in from the Sun.

To find out what those energies are—and what energies affect us—the first thing to look at is the finger length. Do you have long or short fingers? If you start to look at a lot of hands, you will quickly notice that people have fingers that are either long or short. Compare the lengths of the fingers with the palm. If the fingers look almost as long as the palm, they are long fingers. Fingers that look much smaller than the length of the palm are considered short fingers. Now look at your hands or your friend's hands—are the fingers long or short? Don't get your ruler out when you do this. Trust your eyes and your very first thought. Your first guess will almost always be right.

Short Fingers

If you have short fingers, you don't like to sit around for too long. You like to hurry up and get things done. Short-fingered people like to take action. They are the type of people who can not wait to play with the latest gadget. If someone is showing them how to do something, they usually can't wait to try it out. Those who have short fingers like to have many friends. They enjoy being surrounded by active and exciting people. Short-fingered people are also ambitious. If they know what their goals are, they will accomplish them. Laziness is not a quality associated with short fingers, but, if you have short fingers, it may be a good idea to learn patience.

LONG FINGERS

If you have long fingers, you are thoughtful and you like to take your time with things. It's important for you to do things well. You especially do not like to be rushed. Whether you work on a school project or on your own hobby, you like to do things carefully and accurately, and you have an eye for detail. If you draw a tree you will add birds or draw very detailed leaves.

Long-fingered people like to be by themselves much of the time. When they do socialize, they prefer to be with one or two good friends. People with long fingers also get their feelings hurt easily. Do not take other's mean comments seriously.

ETHER: THE ENERGY THAT SURROUNDS OUR HANDS

There are eight Great Elements. They are Earth, Water, Fire, Air, Ether, Mind, Intelligence, and Ego. Four of these are physical, and three are subtle. One is half and half. The physical elements are Earth, Water, Fire, and Air. These physical elements can be experienced through touch, sight, taste, and smell. The subtle elements are Mind, Intelligence, and Ego. They cannot be perceived by our senses because they represent our spirit consciousness, or soul. The element of Ether is on the borderline between being physical and subtle. Sound vibration is actually a product of the etheric world. Sound is carried by air, but is not produced by air, but by the Ether. Everything physically produced in this world begins from sound vibration.

For example, after a plan is conceived by the mind and intelligence, it is carried out into practical reality by the use of speech, words, and discussions. In this way, the element of Ether forms the bridge between consciousness and matter.

This invisible element of Ether surrounds our hands. Place your hands on a table and relax them. Are there spaces between your fingers, or do some of the fingers stay closer together? If there are spaces, it means that the ether is flowing freely around the hand. This is a sign of a strong connection between the mind and the body, which gives the ability to easily carry out plans. Any clinging together of the fingers or thumb to the palm shows that Ether is blocked from that space, limiting its power.

SPACES: If there are spaces between all of your fingers and your thumb, this is a positive indication that your talents are manifesting. Also, the wider the spaces, the more confident and independent the person will be.

CLINGING: If all of your fingers cling closely together, you are definitely holding back your abilities. You are also shy and reserved.

1. Space between the Thumb and the Hand (The Area of Influence):
You have the ability to shape and control situations around you.
Clinging Thumb to the Hand: You find it hard to influence and control the situations around you, and you may have little interest in doing so.

2. Space between the Jupiter and Saturn Fingers (The Area of Action):
You have the ability to act independently and do things on your own when you wish.
Clinging Jupiter and Saturn Fingers: You may be dependent on others and wait for them to take the lead.

3. Space between the Saturn and Sun fingers (The Area of Thought):
You have an independent mind and like to think for yourself. You are not influenced by popular opinion.
Clinging Saturn and Sun Fingers: When making decisions, you are influenced by commonly accepted opinions. You are also concerned with what others think.

4. Space between the Mercury and Sun Fingers (The Area of Communication):
You have the desire and ability to communicate your ideas and opinions.
Clinging Mercury and Sun Fingers: You may be hesitant or reluctant to communicate your thoughts and ideas.

THE SEGMENT GROUPS ON OUR FINGERS

With your palm faced toward you, look at your fingers. You will see that each one of your fingers is divided into three parts, or segments. You will notice three dark horizontal lines that divide each segment from the other. The most important thing to notice is which segment group is the longest. One set of segments, either the upper, middle, or lower will always be longer than the others, even if only slightly.

Again, trust your first quick glance. The more hands that you look at, the easier it will be to recognize which segment group is longer.

The segment groups let us know if we are intellectual, practical, or physical people.

LONG UPPER SEGMENTS

If your upper segments are the longest of the three, you are a thinker. You like to learn and collect information. People with longer uppers like to do things like play chess, read books, and solve puzzles. You also like to be around interesting people who can teach you things and who are full of ideas. You may enjoy history or social studies. News reports are also interesting to you because you like to know what is going on in the world. When you get older, you may want to teach or instruct others in some way.

LONG MIDDLE SEGMENTS

Having the middle segments longest on your fingers show that you are ambitious and like to achieve your goals. When you get older, you may want to become a businessperson because you like money and what it will buy. Longer middles give a person a desire to own and collect things. Adults with long middles like to spend money, especially on things like cars, homes, and jewelry. People with long middles are neat and organized, with a place for everything.

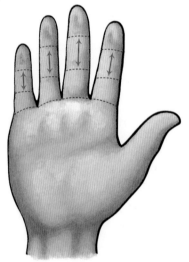

LONG LOWER SEGMENTS

If these are the longest segments of the three for you, then you have a physically strong and healthy body. You will always be active and energetic. It is common among those with long lowers to enjoy working with their hands. This could include fixing things, making things, and cooking.

You will find that you like many things in your life to stay the way they are. For example, you are happy to live in the same house or neighborhood for years. Too much moving and change is very difficult for you. Sticking to a daily schedule will help you to accomplish your goals.

INDIVIDUAL FINGER SEGMENTS

Now we will look closely at each individual finger segment.
Everyone will have one segment that stands out as the longest.
You are now on a mission to find your strongest or most
important finger segment. We call this the main segment.
Your main segment will let you know which are your strongest talents. Examine each of your segments closely and take
your time to discover which of your segments is the longest.
You might want to use a ruler on this one!
When doing this, imagine that each segment
is a piece of chocolate, and you can only
choose one. Which is the largest?
The one that you pick will be your
main segment.

1. UPPER JUPITER: SPIRITUALITY

You are a very spiritual person. You are interested in
all kinds of spiritual activities. You may also have a little
psychic ability.

2. MIDDLE JUPITER: AMBITION

You are ambitious. You like to accomplish big things and rise to the
top. For example, if you're on the track team, you will train harder
than anybody else and be the fastest. You work hard to be the most successful.

25

3. LOWER JUPITER: THE LEADER

You love being in charge of people. Whether you are team captain or class president, you like it when people listen to you. You also have a lot of self-confidence, but watch that you don't become egotistical.

4. UPPER SATURN: KNOWLEDGE

You are an information addict. Learning and studying things is what you love to do. You may enjoy the history channel or reading books on ancient civilizations.

5. MIDDLE SATURN: THE ORGANIZER

You are very good at organizing things. You have the ability to plan group activities and arrange for projects to go smoothly. You probably keep your room very neat and clean.

6. LOWER SATURN: ENVIRONMENTALIST

You love the land, and the earth. You are into ecology and the environment. You can be found outdoors often, and you probably enjoy growing things.

7. UPPER SUN: INDIVIDUALIST

You are an individualist. You do not like to follow the crowd. You add your own personal style to everything that you do. You can also be a risk-taker.

8. MIDDLE SUN: THE ARTIST

Artistic design or decoration is your talent. Everything from computer graphics to arts and crafts interests you. Whether you like to design clothes or draw cartoons, you are a very creative person.

9. LOWER SUN: THE ENTERTAINER

You love to be popular and the center of attention. You tend to be very fashionably dressed. You may want to become an actor or a musician.

10. UPPER MERCURY: THE COMMUNICATOR

You love to talk! You have the ability to express yourself well and might enjoy public speaking. You may also spend a lot of time on the telephone.

11. MIDDLE MERCURY: THE WRITER

You have a natural ability to write. You are very curious and always ask questions. You may be interested in investigative reporting. Write for a newspaper!

12. LOWER MERCURY: TECHNOLOGY

You love all types of technology. This includes electronics and mechanics. Work with computers and gadgets!

FINGERPRINTS: OUR LIFE PATH

Everyone knows that the police use fingerprints to identify people. However, only palmists know that these skin symbols on our fingertips can also tell us our life path. Not even detectives and investigators know this.

Palmistry structures human society according to four different paths of nature. By following our life path, we follow our true nature. Our talents and abilities will quickly come alive when we are aware of our life path.

The life path is your special challenge in this life, something that you did not complete in your previous incarnation. Life will be easier when you follow your life path.

There are four different types of fingerprints. They are:

	THE WAVE Life Path: Responsibility		THE COMET Life Path: The Heart
	THE TENT Life Path: Courage		THE WHIRLPOOL Life Path: The Teacher

Now look closely at all of your fingers, including your thumb. Sometimes fingerprints are hard to see, so hold your fingertips under a bright light. You can use a magnifying glass for this if you need to. In each of

27

the boxes given below, write Wave, Tent, Comet, or Whirlpool for each finger. Remember, each finger can only have one fingerprint.

	Thumb	Jupiter	Saturn	Sun	Mercury
Right Hand					
Left Hand					
	Thumb	Jupiter	Saturn	Sun	Mercury

If you have 2 or more Waves, your life path is Responsibility.
If you have 2 or more Tents, your life path is Courage.
If you have 4 or more Whirlpools, your life path is The Teacher.
If you have 7 or more Comets, your life path is The Heart.

Life Path of Responsibility

Your life path is to be a responsible person. In the duties that are given to you, or that you take on yourself, you will become a strong person by being productive and working hard at what you do. Those that have this life path have difficulty feeling inner peace. They get restless easily if they are not self-disciplined. Even if you have difficulties, you will be able to deal with life easily and stay calm if you take pride in your work and do it well. Also, being in nature makes you feel relaxed. Walking through a forest, working outdoors, or even working in a garden will make you feel happy and fulfilled.

Life Path of the Heart

Your life path is to put your heart into everything that you do. You are happy when you can express your feelings and your dreams. The things that you do the best are the things that you can put your heart and imagination into. Always let others know how you are feeling. If you hide your emotions, life will be very difficult. Also, you may enjoy writing because it is a good way for you to bring out your imaginative ideas and dreams.

Those with the Heart Path tend to be emotional people. Being an emotionally driven person is not a problem, but people on this path worry that if they express their love and feelings for others, they will be rejected. This is rarely how others react, so have the courage to show your feelings and express your love without fear. It takes strength to be loving and honest, so be strong!

Life Path of Courage

Your life path is to always be a go-getter. This means that if you are an enthusiastic person, things will always work out for you. You have the ability to start projects on your own and make things happen. Always remember that things will not go your way if you lack determination or do not take action. You also have the ability to motivate and inspire people—you could organize a large meeting, a protest march, or a charity drive.
This life path provides a special ability to develop the qualities of courage and bravery. So, whether in physical or intellectual activities, never hesitate to take a stand and act boldly.

Life Path of the Teacher

Your life path is to help others to learn. This means that when you are good at something you should share it or teach it to others. For example, if you enjoy playing a sport you should teach others how to play it. If you write a story, you should end it with a message. You are good at coming up with new ideas and sharing them. You like it when people come to you for advice, but you can become upset when they do not listen. This should not discourage you from helping others to learn.
In past ages, those with this life path always held various positions as advisors to the king and queen. You are on the planet to acquire knowledge in order to eventually give guidance and direction to society.

The Thumb

The Thumb: The Lightning Bolt Generator

THE THUMB

Our palm and fingers contain our talents and abilities. Our thumb is like the engine or power station that can make those talents come to life.

PART ONE: THUMB SHAPES

It is only by looking at lots of hands that you will be able to decide if a thumb is fat, thin, long, or short. Don't worry if this part is a bit difficult to figure out. In time, if you look at enough hands, it will be easy. These are the four rules of the thumb:

1. Fat thumbs indicate an outgoing and aggressive nature.

2. Thin thumbs make one quiet and shy.

3. Long thumbs mark one who does things slowly and carefully.

4. Those who do things quickly and immediately have short thumbs.

33

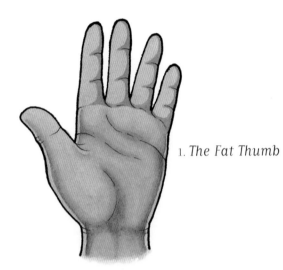

1. *The Fat Thumb*

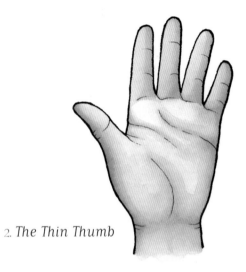

2. *The Thin Thumb*

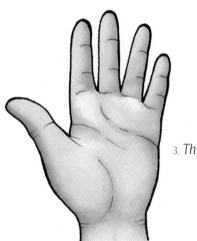

3. *The Long Thumb*

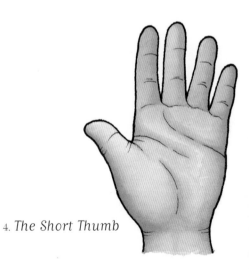

4. *The Short Thumb*

PART TWO: THUMB PLACEMENT

Relax your hands by shaking them. Then place them palm down on a table.
Now look at your thumbs. How far apart do your thumbs stick out from
your palm and fingers?

THUMB PLACEMENT #1

If your thumb sticks way out, you are a very confident person. You like to
depend on yourself and make your own decisions. You especially enjoy being in charge of things and people. You also
like to be a leader. Try not to be too bossy!

THUMB PLACEMENT #2

If your thumb sticks out halfway, you need freedom.
You are not as interested in being in charge of others,
and you like personal independence. It is easy for you
to get along with others. You also like working with a
group or a team.

THUMB PLACEMENT #3

Does your thumb stay close to the palm? If it does it means that you like to keep to yourself
a lot. Actually, you will find that you get things done better when you are alone. Being around
loud people, or people who tell you what to do, is very annoying. Try to be more social or
outgoing if possible. And if you're asked to take on more responsibility, try to do it.

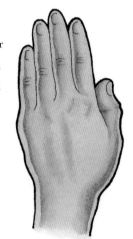

THUMB PLACEMENT #4

When you place your hands down on a table, do your thumbs touch your palms, or even curl within it? You need to become more confident! It is important that you tell your feelings and problems to your parents and those you love and trust. Learn to feel that you can accomplish things if you try hard. Also, try to have a more positive attitude.

PART THREE: THE THREE SEGMENTS OF THE THUMB

(#1) Our thumb is divided into three segments. Which part of your thumb is the longest? If one or two segments are longer than the others, those energies will be stronger for you.

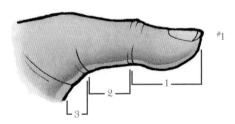

1. THE FIRST SEGMENT: THE SEGMENT OF EGO

The top segment of the thumb represents how much control and influence we have over our environment. This section should be as long or longer than the second segment (#2). It should also feel well-padded and firm to the touch (#3). A segment like this shows the ability to create and shape one's surroundings, and to make things happen. It also gives one the ability to influence others. Segments that are very long or large (#4) show that one can be stubborn and may wish to dominate situations. A strong first segment reveals an ability to achieve results through effort.

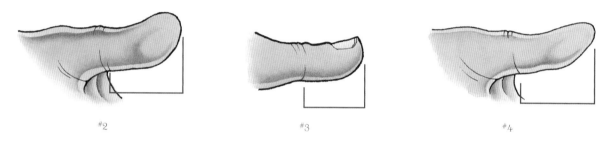

#2   #3   #4

A person with a short or flattened segment (#5) does not have the same ability to have a strong effect on their surroundings. Quite often, the area will also feel soft. This adds to the segment's weakness. A person with a weak segment will feel overwhelmed and frustrated because they have difficulty in achieving results. What if your segment is not strong? You may feel that even if you do work hard at things, success will not come. Learn to break this negative thinking pattern and your first segment will strengthen.

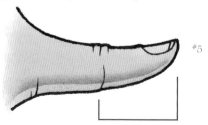

#5

2. THE SECOND SEGMENT: THE SEGMENT OF INTELLIGENCE

The second segment represents the ability to make decisions for yourself. A middle segment that is longer than the other two (#6) reveals that you are constantly thinking about what actions you will take. You also love to give advice to others. You feel good when you are asked to help make choices for others. You are always coming up with plans and ideas. If this segment looks the smallest to you, it means that you are shy about making decisions and plans for yourself. Learn to trust your own decisions and judgments.

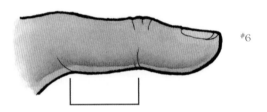

#6

3. THE THIRD SEGMENT OF THE THUMB: THE SEGMENT OF THE MIND

This segment indicates how much determination you have. A good length (#7) shows that you can concentrate your mind on your own personal talents and desires in order to achieve them. It could take the form of a creative or communicative ability. For example, if you have a good imagination, it would be practically applied to some form of art. Or if you have good speaking skills, you would not be afraid to give a speech or express and opinion.

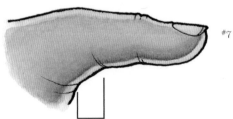

#7

Sometimes this segment is hard to find, or it can look like the thumb has only two segments instead of three (#8). This means that the drive and determination to bring out one's own personal desires and abilities needs to be developed. This particular section of the thumb is the most "changeable" on the hand. If your third segment is weak, remember that goals are easily achieved through making the mind strong by using its powers of concentration. If you do this, your third segment will enlarge.

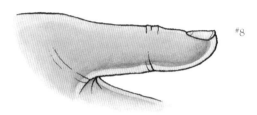

#8

The Lines

The Lines: Rivers of Consciousness

INTRODUCTION TO THE LINES

The lines are created by your brain waves. They are a map of your consciousness. Think of each line as a flowing river. The deeper and wider the line, the more power it can give you.

This means that its energy will be strong in your life.

For example, if your line of Air is deep, it shows that you spend much time in thought (#1).

A shallow or narrow line shows less power in that area. If your line of Air looks light and skinny, it means that you have difficulty concentrating on your plans (#2).

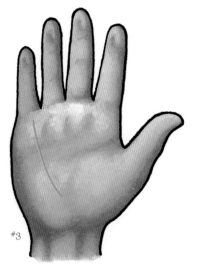

#3

Like a river, a line should also look clear and clean. If it does, it will be easy to express the meaning of that line. For example, if your line of Mercury looks clear, it will be easy for you to communicate your thoughts (#3).

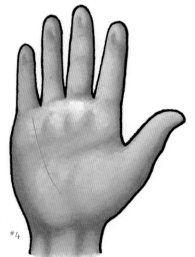

#4

A line can also have its path blocked like a river with many logs or branches in its path. If so, it will be harder to express the energy of that line. For example, a line of Mercury with blockages (crossing lines) will show that you are hesitant to communicate your thoughts (#4).

If you always think of the lines as rivers of energy, understanding them will be easy. Note: when looking at the lines in your palm, remember to concentrate more on your main hand.

THE 14 LINES AND THEIR MEANINGS

The Line of Earth: Lifestyle (Examples #5 - #10)

The Line of Water: Emotions (Ex. #11 - #16)

The Line of Fire: Energy (Ex. #17 - #19)

The Line of Air: Thinking (Ex. #20 - #27)

The Union Line: Focus (Ex. #28)

The Lines of Jupiter: Spirituality (Ex. #29 - #30)

The Line of Saturn: Effort (Ex. #31 - #32)

The Line of the Sun: Optimism (Ex. #33 - #35)

The Line of Mercury: Communication (Ex. #36 - #37)

The Lines of Venus: Enjoyment (Ex. #38 - #39)

The Line of the Moon: Psychic Ability (Ex. #40)

The Lines of Mars: Courage (Ex. #41 - #42)

The Line of Neptune: Sensitivity (Ex. #43)

The Line of Icarus: Freedom (Ex. #44 - #47)

THE LINE OF EARTH

People who know a little bit about palmistry call this line the Life Line. The correct name is the Earth Line. Some people think that this line tells how long a person will live. This is not true. The line of Earth shows how you want to live your life, not how long it will be.

A deep Earth line gives the ability to peacefully handle the difficulties and struggles that one meets in life. A person with a shallow Earth line tends to feel overwhelmed and unsettled when dealing with life's stresses and obstacles. Also keep in mind that the deeper or wider the line of Earth, the more physical strength a person will have. A shallow or narrow line will show a lesser amount of physical strength.

The line of Earth always starts from the middle of the palm (on the thumb side), and moves down the hand. Where the line ends is also very important. The line of Earth curves around the ball of the thumb. That area is called the Mountain of Venus. We will now look at the six basic Earth line patterns. Look at the patterns and discover which Earth line you have. Remember, use your main hand primarily.

THE OUTGOING EARTH LINE

Figure #5 shows an Earth line with a curve that is large and fat. It almost reaches the middle of the palm. This means that you are a very outgoing person. You rarely wish to do things alone, or just be by yourself at home. You most often like to be outside engaged in activities with your friends.

The Line of Earth

#5

THE HOMEBODY EARTH LINE

Figure #6 shows an Earth line that does not curve that far into the palm, but stays close to the thumb. This line will be more straight, rather than forming a curve. This means that being around crowds is not your thing. You like a lot of peace and quiet. You do need to socialize at times, but not too much. You are content with a few good friends.

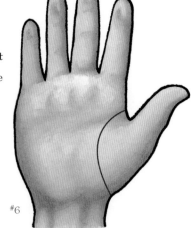

#6

THE FAMILY PERSON EARTH LINE

If your Earth line ends up at the bottom of the Mountain of Venus (#7), you will find that your home and family are extremely important to you. You like a comfortable bedroom and you enjoy decorating it and spending time there. You do not like moving too often. The neighborhood that you live in is also very important to you. You always have a need to know what's going on around your town. When you grow up, you might even want to own a big house in the countryside.

#7

THE ADVENTURER EARTH LINE

This Earth line travels farther toward the other side of the palm. It ends up on the Mountain of the Moon (#8). If the line on your palm does this, you love all types of adventure and travel. You would much rather spend time investigating the world than being around your neighborhood or your home. You might want to become an archaeologist or an explorer. You probably enjoy going on long trips and journeys. Reading about distant places and people also interests you.

THE RESTLESS EARTH LINE

A short Earth line means that a person likes a lot of freedom (#9). Owners of this line are restless and enjoy working hard. If you have this line, you might find that you spend a lot of time and energy working toward a goal. A person training hard for the Olympics may also have this line. Most commonly, those who have this short line will put most of their time and energy into their career. They want to be successful. Sometimes they can work too hard—they need to learn to relax and enjoy themselves.

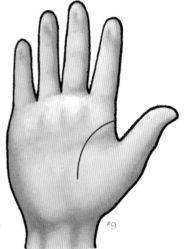

#8

#9

#10

THE CHANGES OF LIFESTYLE EARTH LINE

Example #10 shows a break in the Earth line. This line will travel halfway around the Mountain of Venus and then stop. It will then begin again in a close, but different place. Every time your Earth line breaks, you will move to a different place. If the break is large, you may make a big move that changes your whole life. This may be like moving from the East Coast to the West Coast. If your Earth line has two or three such breaks, it shows that you have the ability to handle these changes.

Remember, this life line shows how you will live your life, not how long you will live. Only God can know that!

THE LINE OF WATER

The line of Water is sometimes called the Heart Line. It is the upper horizontal line on the palm, found just below the fingers. This line always starts from the Mercury finger side of the palm, and travels towards the thumb side. This line tells us about our feelings, our emotions, and what things we put our heart into. The most important thing to notice about this line is whether it is straight or curved (#11 & #12).

Those who have curved Water lines have the ability and the need to express their feelings and emotions (#11). People that have Water lines that are straight also have strong feelings inside, but they have a harder time talking about them (#12).

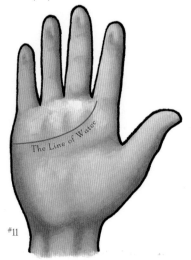
The Line of Water

#11

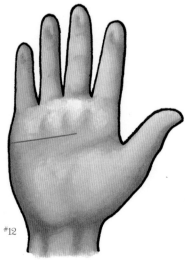

#12

CURVED WATER LINE

(#11) If your Water line curves, you like to express what is in your heart. You have a strong need to always share your feelings and emotions with others. If you like to write, the topics tend to be about who and what you love. If something is bothering you, you need to let others know about it and not hold it in.

SRAIGHT WATER LINE

(#12) When you talk to others, you express what is going on in your mind rather than your heart.
You may have difficulty discussing your feelings with others, but you are comfortable expressing your thoughts and ideas. Try not to be shy about letting other people know how you are feeling, rather than just what you are thinking.

Now we will look at four of the most important Water line endings. Look at your palm to see which one of these you have.

THE STRAIGHT SATURN WATER LINE

(#13) You put your feelings and emotions into becoming a strong, self-confident, and independent person. You enjoy working alone, rather than with others. You are able to get more things done when you do things by yourself. You are a very independent person, and you like to have freedom. You do need to socialize sometimes, but not as much as others. You're the type of person that loves to have your own special private place. It is hard for you to express your feelings to others. Do not be shy about expressing them from time to time. You do have a warm heart, but you hold back and keep a lot inside. If you do not express your feelings at all, you will feel that others don't understand you.

#13

SATURN

THE CURVED SATURN WATER LINE

(#14) You put your feelings and emotions into enjoying life, being active, and becoming a leader. When you do things with other people, you like to be the leader of the group. You also do not like to follow the rules of others. Your friends will listen to what you have to say when you are in charge. You also like to be the center of attention. You get bored very easily if you are around dull and uninteresting people. You like to attend loud parties and amusement parks, and play challenging sports.

THE CURVED JUPITER WATER LINE

(#15) Your feelings and emotions are put into your friends and those who you love. In order for you to get things done, it is important for you to work in a peaceful and quiet area. You like to work with others, but only if it is with people that you know very well. You prefer to work in small groups. Getting along with people is important to you, and you hate fighting and arguing. You can be a very dependable friend, and you expect your friends to be loyal to you. When someone around you is sick or needs some kind of help, you're always there for them. Many people who love and care for animals also have this Water line pattern.

THE STRAIGHT JUPITER WATER LINE

(#16) You will put your emotions and feelings into helping humanity.
You love working with large groups of people. You always enjoy meeting new people and making friends. It

is easy for you to share and cooperate with others. You are also good at bringing people together. You will find that your friends will easily tell you their feelings and problems. This Water line pattern makes you able to give good advice, and you love doing it! This is because you have a talent for analyzing the world of emotions. Many psychologists have this shape of Water line. People who become doctors, healers, or astrologers also have this line because they enjoy helping others.

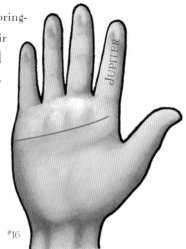

#16

THE LINE OF FIRE

This is one of the most important lines in your palm. This line sits just behind the Earth line (#17). Fire itself attracts us. It is bright, intense, and always moving. A blazing fire draws us in like a magnet. Therefore, anyone who has this line will be full of life. You want to be with them because they are fun and exciting to be with.

People who have a line of Fire have the element of fire within them. This fire energy makes a person always active and busy. This line does not give physical energy—that's the job of the Earth line—but it gives more of a restless energy. Just as fire is always restless and does not want to stay in one place, owners of this line can't stay still for very long.

They always have to be doing something. You do not need to have a long and deep line of Fire to own this fire energy. Most people will have one or two little pieces of it.

This line is so powerful that you only need a very small part of it for it to do its job. One small flame can start a giant fire (#18).

A deep line of Fire can make you an enthusiastic person and motivated to accomplish things (#19). It gives one the needed energy to get things going. Think of a stick of dynamite: It has the power to cause a large explosion, but it's harmless without the strike of a match. The Fire line is like our match. Some people do not have any trace of this line. This means that they may have the desire or the physical strength to do things but they may be lazy or uninspired. Having a Fire line will give one the needed energy to get things started. If you see a friend who does not seem to have this line, encourage them to become more enthusiastic. If they do, the line will slowly begin to appear.

#18

The Line of Earth

The Line of Fire ←

#19 ←

THE LINE OF AIR

(#20) The line of Air is the horizontal line in the middle of the palm.

It starts from the thumb side of the hand, and travels toward the Mercury finger side. Air (or wind) carries sound, which carries information and ideas. For example, man and most animals communicate their thoughts and ideas by sound, which is carried by the air. So, this line of Air carries our thoughts, ideas, and interests. It explains how we think and what we think about. There are two parts to this section: Part One talks about the shape of the line, Part Two about the length. So, if our brain is a computer, then the shape of the line shows us

#20

The Line of Air

The Line of Earth

what kind of computer we own. The length of the line will show us how we use our computer.

Part One: Air Line Shapes

There are four main Air line shapes. Look at them all, and decide which one you have.

The Straight Line of Air

(#21) Does your line of Air travel straight? If so, you are a logical thinker. You base a lot of your thinking and views on facts and information. For you to believe in something, it has to be proven to you. You are very good at analyzing things. You will find this line on many scientific researchers and inventors.

This straight line is also common on those who enjoy working with technology and mathematical formulas. Owning this line means that you like to read things that give you information and knowledge. You like non-fiction and how-to books. If you like a book of fiction at all, it usually has to be based on true-life events. You also have the ability to observe and study facts. Most detectives have this type of line.

#21

The Curved Line of Air

(#22) Does your line of Air curve down slightly? If so, you are a creative thinker. You base a lot of your thinking upon how you would like or wish things to be. You have many original ideas. People who have curved Air

#22

lines enjoy being artists, musicians, and actors. Many movie directors also have this line pattern. This is also an indicator of a person who can design and create things such as clothes, cars, and houses.

You also love variety in your life! For example, you may meet people who only like a certain type of music, and no other. If you like music, you will enjoy listening to everything. You have a very open mind and can be inspired by many different things.

THE STRONGLY CURVED LINE OF AIR

(#23) Does your line of Air strongly curve down? If so, you have a strong and colorful imagination. You spend much time dreaming, night and day. If you try writing or drawing, you could create amazing fantasy. Many science fiction, romance, and fantasy artists and writers have this type of line. There is also a moody side to you. When you feel moody, you will learn a lot about yourself by writing down your thoughts.

There is also a very spiritual side to you. It is easy for you to accept that there is a God and spiritual forces. You are always on the lookout to see spiritual reasons behind things that take place. You are not the type who believes that things just happen by chance. People with this line also become interested in legends from the ancient world, such as Greek or Egyptian mythologies.

You have the ability to trust an inner voice. This is a feeling from inside that lets you know what you should or should not do. Trust this voice. If you listen to it, it can help you to make the right decisions. This feeling is called intuition.

THE CURVED UP LINE OF AIR

(#24) Does your line of Air curve up? If so, you are a practical thinker. You think in a very down-to-earth way.

The Line of Air

#23

Things have to be realistic, and not imaginative. For example, you like art that shows things the way they are, not someone's fantasy. You have a very sharp or shrewd mind. This means that if you have to buy something, you would make sure to get the best price, and you rarely get cheated. This pattern also shows an ability to make money and spend it wisely. People with this line are great at starting new companies and businesses. You will see it on bankers and successful business people.

You would love being part of a debate team. You have the ability to completely understand the other person's point of view, and then defeat them, using their own argument! That is why the best lawyers always have this line.

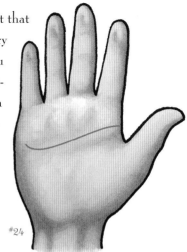

#24

Part Two: Air Line Lengths

There are three main Air line lengths. Look at them all, and decide which one you have.

Air Line Ending Within Section A
(Under the Finger of Saturn)

(#25) If your Air line ends within section A, your mind thinks in the present. When deciding to do something, you trust the first thought that comes to you, or your first idea. You are not interested in what has happened in the past, and you will deal with the future when it comes. Therefore, you have the ability to make decisions immediately and you can give quick answers. When asked a question, you almost never say "maybe" or "give me time to think about it." And if someone insults you, you will always have a fast comeback line.

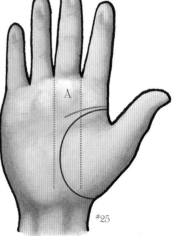

A

#25

AIR LINE ENDING WITHIN SECTION B
(UNDER THE FINGER OF THE SUN)

(#26) Those who have the section B ending put a lot of thought into making plans for the future. For example, if they earn money, they will not spend it immediately. They will take time to think about how they are going to spend it, and they may even save it. If you have this Air line length, you will put a lot of time training or working toward a future goal. This could be something like practicing on an instrument or training for a sport for several hours a day. You like to have fun, but you will always be very serious about your future ambitions.

#26

AIR LINE ENDING WITHIN SECTION C
(UNDER THE FINGER OF MERCURY)

(#27) If you have the section C ending, you make your decisions based upon your past experiences. If asked a question, you will always think about your answer carefully. This is because you consider experiences that have happened in the past when deciding what to do in the future. You don't like to be rushed into making plans. You have a mind that can take in a lot of information. Therefore, you put a lot of thought into the things that you do.

The Line of Air

#27

THE UNION LINE

Occasionally, you will find a palm that shows the Air Line and the Heart Line merged together (#28). It is not uncommon to find this line, but it is rare to find it on both palms.

When lines are separated and do not touch each other, they have the ability to bring out their full power. Lines that begin and end independently act like radars. Just as a radar can send out and pick up signals and information, an independent line can properly express and receive energies. A line that runs into or combines with another line will lose this radar-like ability.

A person with such a line has difficulty communicating their internal thoughts and feelings. This is combined with having a lack of ability to understand the psychology of others. Relating to people and forming strong friendships is a challenge for them. They find it easier to stay in their own world and consequently, they often end up feeling lonely and isolated.

If you have this line, take the time to inquire about the thoughts and feelings of your friends. Make more of an effort to clearly explain what is going on inside of you. If you do this, you will feel much more harmony in your life.

The Union Line does have a positive side. Those with it have the ability to focus and concentrate on a goal without letting anything distract them. You will find this line on successful politicians, entertainer, and business people who do not let anything get in the way of achieving their goals. When the Air and Water lines run together, one becomes emotionally involved in everything that one thinks about. The result is that such people are able to strongly focus on their interests because the mind and the heart act as one.

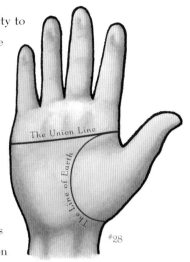

THE LINES OF JUPITER

The Lines of Jupiter are lines of Spiritual and Mystical Awareness. These lines can be found on the upper part of the Mountain of Jupiter, just below the finger of Jupiter (#29). They will usually be narrow and short. Look at this area very closely. These lines can be very light and difficult to see. Any lines in this area are lines of spirituality. If you have them, it means that you had an interest in mystical or spiritual things in your past lives.

What if you have one strong line directly under the finger of Jupiter (#30)? This means that in your past lives, you prayed to and worshiped God as a person, rather than as an energy or a "force."

If you continue your spiritual path, these lines will get longer, deeper, and stronger. What if you do not have any lines in this area? Do not worry, they will appear and grow if you become interested in a spiritual path.

The Lines of Jupiter →

#30

THE LINE OF SATURN: THE LINE OF EFFORT

This line starts out at the bottom of the palm, and travels toward the finger of Saturn (#31). It is easy to find because it is the vertical line that runs through the center of the palm. It will not always be a straight line. This line shows that one has the ability to make an effort. The person will try very hard to accomplish things. It is a very important line to have. If you have this line, it means that you take time to do things that need to be done. You work at things that are expected of you, like school or your duties at home. This can also include a hobby that you work hard at. You may sometimes see palms that do not have a Saturn line, or it may be so light and narrow that it is hard to see (#32).

The Line of Saturn

#31

#32

This means that the person does not try hard enough at what needs to be done or what is expected of them. They may waste a lot of their time or relax too much. If you see someone without this important line, encourage them to be more serious about their responsibilities.

THE LINE OF THE SUN: THE LINE OF OPTIMISM

This line appears on the Mountain of the Sun, under the finger of the Sun. It is usually found above the line of Water (#33). It is usually not very long. There can also be a bunch of short Sun lines in the same space (#34). This will almost be the same as having one line.

This line does not have to be strongly cut into your palm. This is a powerful line, and you only need to have a small bit of it in order for the Sun energy to come through. Do not worry if your line (or lines) are light and narrow. The Sun makes us happy and joyful when it shines brightly on us, especially if it has been dark and cloudy for a long time.

The line of Sun gives us this bright Sun energy. Having this line means that you are able to be positive. Those with a Sun line do not get discouraged or disappointed easily. Even if they are having a bad day, they do not let it get them down for very long. They just know that everything will soon work out for them. If you have a Sun line, you are able to help your friends feel better when they are feeling sad or upset.

Just as you cannot ignore the Sun on a hot day, those owning a Sun line naturally attract people. They are noticed and remembered. If you ever have the chance to read the hands of popular entertainers, check out their Sun line. The longer and deeper

The Line of the Sun

The Line of Water

#33

#34

their line, the longer they will stay popular (#35).

What if you have no Sun line at all? Try to develop a positive attitude, and never give up. Learn to see that any difficulties that you go through should not discourage you, but help to make you a stronger person. If you do this, the line of Sun will start to grow on your hand.

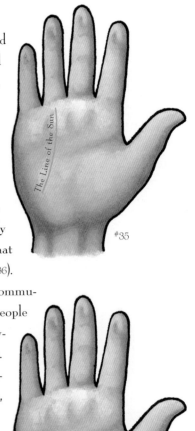

#35

THE LINE OF MERCURY:
THE LINE OF COMMUNICATION

The line of Mercury is found on the Mercury finger side of the palm. It is easy to identify because it is the only vertical line that heads toward the finger of Mercury (#36).

The line shows that you can and want to communicate through writing and speaking. Many people can communicate or speak well, but not everybody has a strong need to express their own views. If you have this line, being able to express your opinions is very important to you. Most people, for example, will be able to tell you what they heard on a news report, but a person with a Mercury line will give you the news—and their opinion on it.

What if you have a Mercury line, but it is broken up or very light (#37)? This means that you want to express your opinions but you hold back. This is because you feel that people will not take your thoughts or opinions seriously. Don't worry about this; express your ideas to people anyway, and your line will grow strong and deep.

#36

#37

What if there is no line of Mercury on your hand? Writing might be a good way to form your opinions and thoughts.

THE LINES OF VENUS: THE LINES OF ENJOYMENT

The lines of Venus are short horizontal lines on the Mountain of Venus. On this area, you might have three or four strong lines or many little ones (#38).

These lines mean that you love to play around, laugh, and enjoy yourself. You also like to entertain others, go to parties, and socialize. You will have a serious side, but you also need to have fun. The more lines of Venus that you have, the more enjoyment you will seek out. So if the Mountain is completely covered with Venus lines, the person will be a party animal (#39).

If the Venus lines are hard to find, it means that the enjoying spirit is not very strong. Therefore they may rarely be interested in socializing and playing around.

The Line of Earth

The Mountain of Venus

The Lines of Venus

#38

#39

THE LINE OF THE MOON: THE LINE OF PSYCHIC ABILITY

(#40) This line usually forms a half-circle on the Mountain of the Moon. To have it means that you have true psychic power. You may have the ability to know what will happen in the future. Owners of the line of the Moon seem to know who is calling

The Line of the Moon

The Mountain of the Moon

#40

them when the phone rings. It can give one the power to read others thoughts or know what people are going to say before they say it. If you have this line, try working with the Tarot cards and your psychic ability may become strong.

THE LINES OF MARS: THE LINES OF BEING BOLD

These lines start out on the Mountain of Mars and move out into the rest of the palm (#41). These lines make one competitive and aggressive. People who own deep Mars lines use their competitiveness in a physical way. You will find these lines on professional athletes. If the Mars lines are very deep, they show one who is courageous and brave. Firefighters and policemen have very deep Mars lines.

Mars lines that are more shallow and narrow (#42) belong to people who are competitive and aggressive with their mind and thoughts. They can use this competitive energy in a career such as news reporting, politics, and business. When you see these lines of Mars, remember that they add an extra measure of boldness to a person's life.

THE LINE OF NEPTUNE: THE LINE OF SENSITIVITY

(#43) The line of Neptune is a small half-circle line at the very top of the palm. Having this line on your palm shows that you are always warm and friendly to others. You are also sensitive to the world around you. The people around you or the places you go often influence your moods. It also bothers you to see people or animals suffer. Therefore, you will want a career in which you can help others. You may even enjoy working with animals. Arguments and fights disturb those with the line of Neptune; they are pleased when people around them cooperate and work together.

THE LINE OF ICARUS: THE LINE OF FREEDOM

In ancient Greek mythology, the demigods Icarus and his father, Daedalus, escaped from prison by using wings made of wax. As Daedalus flew on to Sicily, Icarus flew so high that the sun melted his wings and he fell to earth. This line is named after Icarus because it symbolizes a need for freedom and excitement. As human beings, we need to know that we have a certain amount of freedom and independence in our lives in order to be happy and peaceful. Those with the line of Icarus have a constant need to break free from restrictions and limitations imposed upon them.

The Line of Icarus

#44

They may also constantly push themselves to do things better than they have before. They strongly dislike living in a society that limits their freedom. They value independence and rarely follow the crowd unless it suits their own desire. They are never people who become blind followers, going along with what is commonly accepted.

There are four types of Icarus lines:

The lines in example #44 start from the edge of the Moon Mountain. They are short lines usually about one inch in length. Having one to four lines shows that the person likes a life

The Line of Icarus

The Line of Saturn

#45

63

in which they can have a different schedule every day. They do not like routines. A person with five or more lines gets bored very easily and likes constant change. They enjoy traveling and visiting new places. If the line of Icarus starts from the Moon Mountain and connects to the Saturn line, as in #45, it is one's career that must be both adventurous and exciting. It can be found on those who plan events around the world or set up archaeological research sites. Traveling and exploring will usually be a big part of their job, and they may even search for some type of buried treasure.

In example #46, the Icarus line starts from the Moon Mountain and connects to the Earth line. This shows a strong need to engage in physical activities that are challenging and even experimental. They are risk-takers and thrill seekers. These people may be found hang gliding, racing cars, and climbing difficult mountains. Example #47 shows an Icarus line that curves almost in a semicircle. It may reach the beginning edges of the Venus Mountain. These people need mental or intellectual freedom. They may be found writing or speaking out against the government or hosting a radio talk show where they can offer views and opinions that question popular culture or thinking. If you have any form of the Icarus line, you will be most happy when you throw off conformity and live an exciting and interesting life.

HOW TO READ A HAND QUICKLY

This last section will show you how to do a quick palmistry reading. In this type of reading, we will only use the Earth, Water, and Air lines. Look at these three lines, and decide which one of the three stands out the most. It will look the deepest and the darkest, and it will draw your eyes to it. By looking at which line stands out, you will be able to know which basic direction a person's life will take.

If the Earth line is the strongest (#48):
The world of physical activities is most interesting to this person. They enjoy sports and being outdoors. They will have a strong physical body. They love to build things and may even have a career in construction. Anyone who uses their body a great deal, from athletes to farmers, will have a strong Earth line.

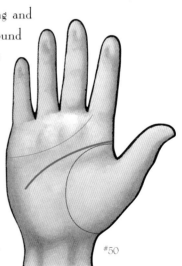

The Line of Water
The Line of Air
The Line of Earth

#48

If the Water line is the strongest (#49):
This person will be very friendly and easy to be around. The world of the heart and emotions is most important to them. They are usually caring and generous. They need to have peace around them and work in a quiet area. These people like to get into activities in which they can bring out their feelings and the feelings of others.

#49

If the Air line is the strongest (#50):
This person will spend most of their time using their mind. They are constantly thinking, and they love collecting information and knowledge. They like to know what is going on in the world, along with the latest news and events. They may be interested in science, research, and philosophy.

#50

How to Give a Palmistry Reading

- You and your "querent"—the person who is getting a reading from you—should sit across from each other.

- You should both be very comfortable and relaxed.

- Ask the querent if they are right-handed or left-handed. Look at both hands, but most of your attention should be on their main hand. The main hand is the right hand for right-handers and the left hand for left-handers.

- To read a hand properly, you need enough light. You can read a hand in the sunlight, or you can use a table lamp.

- It is always better to read the querent's hand in a quiet and private area. Do palmistry in a place where you will not be disturbed.

- A palmist is always silent after a reading. Never tell others what you have seen on a person's hand even if their friends ask you! A reading is only between you and the querent. It is private.

- If you start to read hands regularly, buy a small magnifying glass. Palmists are never without their magnifying glass.

- Tell your querent only what you see on their hands. Never make anything up! Remember that people never forget the words of a palmist, so be truthful.

- The last and most important rule in palmistry: Read hands to help people. Never do it to show off!

Closing Remarks

I hope that this book has inspired you to read hands, and you continue to explore the path of palmistry. Hand-reading is a fascinating art, and there is no limit to how much you can discover.

Remember that palmistry can only be learned by regular practice. It is not just "book knowledge."

The more you look at hands, the more your skill and abilities will develop. In time, your confidence will grow, and palmistry will feel very natural and comfortable to you. William Benham, the great American palmist, once wrote, "Palmistry is a study worthy of the best efforts of the best minds."

I recommend the following books:

1. *Palmistry* by Sasha Fenton and Malcolm Wright (Crescent)

2. *Palmistry: The Whole View* by Judith Hipskind (Llewllyn)

3. *Practical Palmistry* by David Brandon-Jones (CRCS Publishing)

4. *The Complete Book of the Hand* by Lori Reid (Pan Books)

5. *Hand Psychology* by Andrew Fitzherbert (Avery Publishing)

6. *The Hand Reveals* by Dylan Warren-Davis (Element Books)

7. *The Benham Book of Palmistry* by William G. Benham (Newcastle)

About the Author

 Vernon Mahabal is the founder and director of the Palmistry Institute in San Francisco. In 1979 he began formal training in Vedic (Eastern) cosmology, which took him to India many times. He combines Western astrological palmistry with Chinese elemental hand analysis. He also continues new research, particularly within the field of fingerprints (dermatoglyphics). Mahabal has read thousands of hands, given hundreds of lectures, and trained hundreds of students to read hands.

Vernon hosted his own national cable show called *The Palmistry Show with Vernon Mahabal* and has given numerous radio interviews. He has written many articles on palmistry for various periodicals and has also been consulted by the *New York Daily News*.

The objectives of the Palmistry Institute are to further new advances in the field of hand analysis and to serve as a research and information resource. Its purpose is to restore the practice of palmistry to its rightful place as a respected and esteemed science. Vernon Mahabal can be reached at www.palmistryinstitute.com.

Acknowledgments

SPIRITUAL INSPIRATIONS

Srila Narayana Maharaja, Srila Satsvarupa Maharaja, Srila Prabhupada, Sri Sri Radha-Govinda.

FAMILY & FRIENDS

Mom, Syamala, Tirthapada, Jaya Sri Clark, Jahnava Edwards, Charles Chan, Valerie Clark & Aaron Mishkin, Carrie, Arleen & Warren Butterworth, Noel dela Merced, Nancy & Augustine Reyes, Jill & Mark Koperweis, Donald De Voe, Wendy & Ronald Smith, Alana & Richard Unger, J. Owen Swift.

INSPIRATIONS

William G. Benham, Ludwig Van Beethoven, Black Sabbath, Trouble, Iron Maiden, Sleep, Judas Priest, Dr. Michael Savage.

Extra special thanks to Jill Tabler-Koperweis for proofreading and much encouragement.

Design by Mandala Design Group

Art Direction by N. D. Koster, Cover by Jonathan Hebel, Design & Layout by Andrea Di Falco & Alan Hebel.

Illustrations by Kamala Dolphin-Kingsley.